T0084306

Baroque Dances

for descant recorder
with additional 2ⁿᵈ part

edited by
Rainer Butz and Hans Magolt

ED 20652-01
ISMN 979-0-001-17862-4

Cover: Karin Schliehe and Bernhard Mark

Composers on the cover:
G. F. Händel (top left), J. S. Bach (top middle),
C. Monteverdi (top right), H. Purcell (bottom left), J. B. Lully (bottom right)

www.schott-music.com

Mainz · London · Berlin · Madrid · New York · Paris · Prague · Tokyo · Toronto
© 2011 SCHOTT MUSIC GmbH & Co. KG, Mainz · Printed in Germany

2

Branle simple and Branle gay

De Post (Danserye, Antwerp 1551)

♩ = ca. 72, Introduction: 2 bars

Tielman Susato
~1500-1561

Arrangements: Rainer Butz

Branle gay

Branle double

Bransle (Terpsichore, Wolfenbüttel 1612)

♩ = ca. 68, Introduction: 2 bars with upbeat

Michael Praetorius
1571-1621

Branle gay
(Neuf basses dances deux branles etc., Paris 1530)

Pierre Attaingnant
~1494-1551

$\downarrow. =$ ca. 68, Introduction: 4 bars with upbeat

Basse dance

(Neuf basses dances deux branles etc., Paris 1530)

Pierre Attaingnant
~1494-1551

♩ = ca. 116, Introduction: 2 bars

Ronde and Saltarelle

Ronde and Hupfauf (Danserye, Antwerp 1551)

Tielman Susato
~1550-1561

♩ = ca. 128, Introduction: 2 bars

Saltarelle

6

Basse dance

La mourisque / Moorish dance (Danserye, Antwerp 1551)

Tielman Susato
~1500-1561

𝅗𝅥 = ca. 80, Introduction: 2 bars

Basse dance and after-dance

Bergerette „Dont vient cela" and Reprise (Danserye, Antwerp 1551)

Tielman Susato
~1500-1561

♩ = ca. 144, Introduction: 6 crotchets

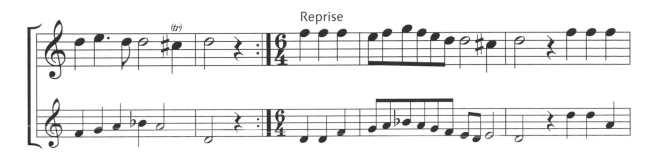

Reprise

Pavane and Galliarde

Belle qui tiens ma vie (Orchésographie, Langres 1589)

♩ = ca. 102, Introduction: 4 bars

Thoinot Arbeau
1520-1595

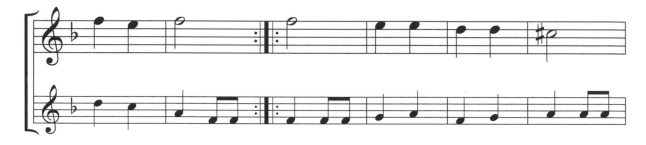

Galliarde

Pavane

Pavane de Spaigne (Terpsichore, Wolfenbüttel 1612)

Michael Praetorius
1571-1621

♩ = ca. 64, Introduction: 2 bars

Galliarde

Galiarda (Fitzwilliam Virginal Book, ~1550-1620)

John Bull
~1562-1628

♩ = ca. 160, Introduction: 2 bars

10

Pavane

Pavan of my Lord Lumley (Fitzwilliam Virginal Book, ~1550-1620)

John Bull
~1562-1628

♩ = ca. 52, Introduction: 2 bars

Galliarde

Wer wird mich herzen (Lute Book)

Johan Thysius
1621-1653

♩ = ca. 168, Introduction: 2 bars

Galliarde

Dancing and jumping (Lustgarten neuer teutscher Tänze, 1601)

Hans Leo Haßler
1562-1612

♩ = ca. 172, Introduction: 2 bars

Dance and after-dance

in the style of Allemande and Tripla (Nuremberg ~1600)

Valentin Haußmann
~1570-1614

♩ = ca. 144, Introduction: 2 bars with upbeat

After-dance

Siciliana
Moresca from the opera „L'Orfeo" (1607)

Claudio Monteverdi
1567-1643

♩. = ca. 56, Introduction: 2 bars with upbeat

Allemande and Tripla

(Banchetto musicale, Leipzig 1617)

Johann Hermann Schein
1586-1630

♩ = ca. 140, Introduction: 2 bars with upbeat

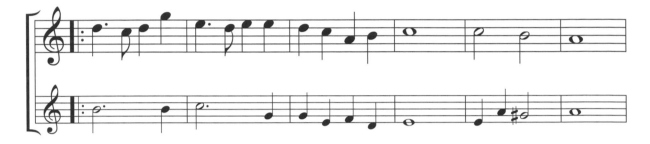

Tripla

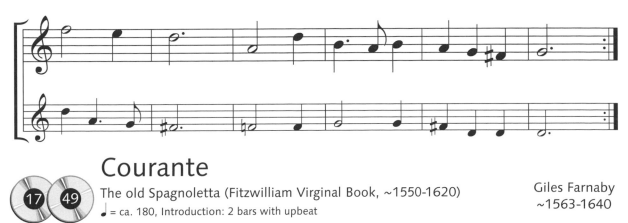

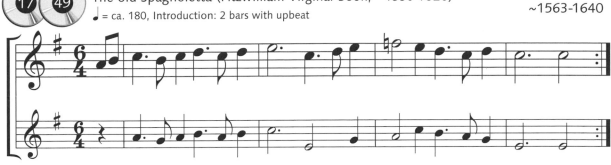

Courante

The old Spagnoletta (Fitzwilliam Virginal Book, ~1550-1620)

Giles Farnaby
~1563-1640

♩ = ca. 180, Introduction: 2 bars with upbeat

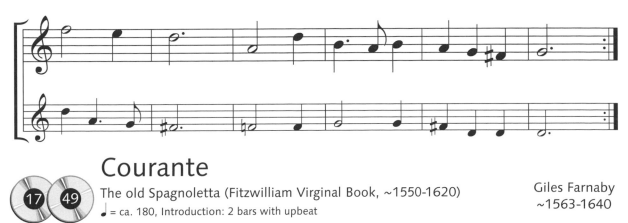

16

Allemande

18 **50** Nun will der Lenz uns grüßen (before 1600)

♩ = ca. 120, Introduction: 2 bars with upbeat

adapted from an old
German round-dance song

Courante

19 **51** Wie schön blüht uns der Maien

♩. = ca. 56, Introduction: 2 bars with upbeat

Heidelberger Liederblatt
1602

Courante

20 52
in Michael Praetorius (Terpsichore, Wolfenbüttel 1612)

Pierre Francisque Caroubel
~1560-1611

♩. = ca. 60, Introduction: 2 bars with upbeat

Sarabande

21 53
from the Suite in D minor for harpsichord HWV 437 (before 1733)

Georg Friedrich Händel
1685-1759

♩ = ca. 68, Introduction: 2 bars with 3 upbeat crotchets

Sarabande

Aria „Lascia ch'io pianga" from the opera „Rinaldo" (1711)

Georg Friedrich Händel
1685-1759

♩ = ca. 68, Introduction: 2 bars with 1 upbeat crotchet

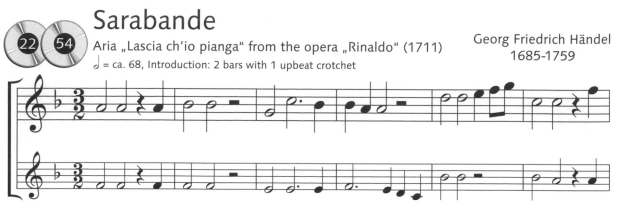

Fine

D.C. al Fine

Gigue

23 **55** Down the green fields, we'll jig it

English folk tune

♩. = ca. 64, Introduction: 2 bars

Fine

D.C. al Fine con rip.

Gigue

24 **56** Ich spring' an diesem Ringe

Lochamer Liederbuch
~1452-1460

♩. = ca. 60, Introduction: 2 bars with upbeat

Sarabande

Air tendre for harpsichord

Jean-Baptiste Lully
1632-1687

♩ = ca. 68, Introduction: 2 bars

March

Funeral march from the oratorio „Saul" (1739)

♩ = ca. 60, Introduction: 1 bar with upbeat

Georg Friedrich Händel
1685-1759

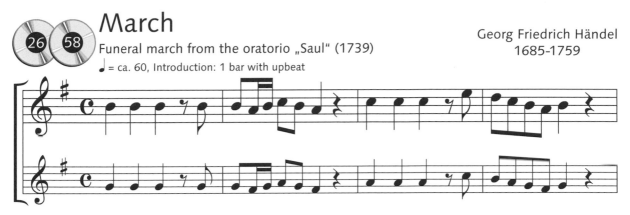

Minuet

Aria „How blest are shepherds" from the opera „King Arthur" (1691)

Henry Purcell
1659-1695

♩ = ca. 112, Introduction: 2 bars

Minuet

(Clavierbüchlein for Anna Magdalena Bach, Leipzig 1725, BWV Anh.114)

Christian Petzold
1677-1733

♩ = ca. 112, Introduction: 2 bars

Chaconne

from the opera „The Fairy Queen" (1692)

Henry Purcell
1659-1695

♩ = ca. 76, Introduction: 2 bars

Passepied
from the opera „L'Europe galante" (1697)

André Campra
1660-1744

♪ = ca. 152, Introduction: 2 bars with upbeat

Gavotte
from the Orchestral Suite No. 3 in D major BWV 1068 (1731)

Johann Sebastian Bach
1685-1750

♩ = ca. 60, Introduction: 2 bars with 2 upbeat crotchets

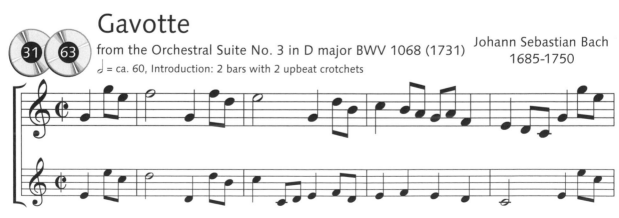

Hornpipe

Duet „Shepherd leave decoying" from the opera „King Arthur" (1691)

Henry Purcell
1659-1695

♩ = ca. 76, Introduction: 2 bars

Pavane (Abraham Bosse 1635)

Louis XIV dances a minuet (Pierre Landry 1682)

Sarabande (from Gregorio Lambranzi: Neue und Curieuse Theatralische Tantz=Schul, Nuremberg 1716)

Contents

Baroque fingering chart

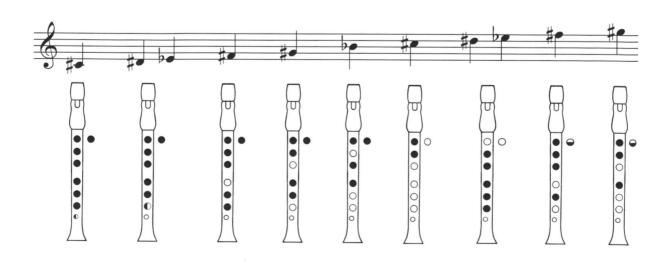

Minuet (from Pierre Rameau: Le maître à danser, Paris 1734)

Reverence (Christoph Murer, around 1600)

Reverence (from Th. Arbeau: Orchésographie, 1589)